Whitepap‹

I0019787

Data Center Convergence

Overcoming the Fatal Flaw

Written by:
Randy Chalfant – Fellow

With Forwards by:
Steve O'Donnell – Partner
Barry Rudolph – Fellow

ISBN-13: 978-1481142601
ISBN-10: 1481142607

International Advisory Board Professionals

Forward

Steve O'Donnell

For the CEO, IT is delivered in a sub-optimal way. IT platforms themselves need to be replaced very frequently (compared to other capital equipment life-cycles) yet these same platforms resist changes to the scale, scope and capability of the business processes and applications they support. Inflexible operations combined with high maintenance, a very bad combination.

For the CIO, technology stuff doesn't stay around long enough to mature properly. Just as he was getting used to mainframes, along came client-server and workstation based systems and everything had to change, new people skills, new business processes and new technology.

Whilst technology advances are useful, can deliver good ROI and enable companies to compete better, they are costly and risky transitions to deliver. In summary, IT moves too fast - massive leaps in capability often driven by the neatness of the technology rather than driven by a real business problem.

We are on the threshold of a new IT paradigm, Converged Infrastructure (also known variously as Cloud Computing, Software Defined Data Centre and Infrastructure as a Service), that delivers the promise of flexibility and low maintenance, as well as offering benefits in terms of ROI and agility.

The question we need to ask ourselves is this yet another disruption that will take a decade to deliver whilst creating huge risk and cost in its wake?

So what is Converged Infrastructure and why is it important and different?

New type of IT - no longer IT Separates - converged or cloud. Value moves to software

What are the implications of converged?

How is this going to work?

The global scale of today's IT workloads, combined with Moore's Law growth in CPU performance and high degrees of virtualization have led to massive resource demands on the network and storage layers.

This unique book will help you position the events leading up to the delivery of IT as a Service, the constraints that are moving aside to enable converged infrastructure.

Barry Rudolph

There are significant changes in progress in the way in which IT is delivered, how it is used and consumed, and by whom it is consumed. The drivers are relentless. Massive growth in scale, including the number of users, their geographic locality, huge growth in the amount, type and velocity of data, and the increasing desire to not only provide access and safety, but create value for the company and it's customers from the data.

The ability to rethink the manner in which infrastructure is provided is also being enabled through significant growth in network bandwidths, ever increasing compute power through both basic semiconductor improvements as well as multi-core technology, and new memory technology providing very fast and efficient persistent storage.

It is an amazing set of never ending advancements driving new innovations in both the base offerings of compute, storage, networking and management, but more importantly enabling whole new technical and business architectures.

These new architectures include hyper-scale clustering and distributed systems, highly virtualized environments to improve agility, efficiency and utilization and more highly integrated and converged systems, clouds and software defined data centers.

These newer approaches promise dramatic improvements in efficiency, significant increases in flexibility and agility, and an ease of management that will help mask the incredible challenge of managing these huge and complex environments.

So, why write an book on the topic? Let's just get on with execution and deliver improved business results to the company while simplifying the life of the CIO? Easy – right?

Well, not so fast. These new architectural paradigms put significant stress in specific areas of the technology and design. These stresses can cause execution and management risk, but frankly there is always risk in new innovations. The real issue is that there are areas of converged systems, that if not addressed ahead of time can become a show-stopper!

This book takes a very methodical approach to describing the drivers, the architectural choices, and very importantly, identifying the stress or breaking points so that you can deal with them ahead of time and not as your project is in crisis.

Whether you are a business executive exploring the benefits of utilizing these new IT delivery methods or a technology executive responsible for the decision-making and execution, take the time to read through this book and gain the insight that it will provide.

Introduction

The Vision

Industry related marketing departments are burning the midnight oil to create the most insightful, dramatic, and compelling strategy and market position related to the giant next new wave in the Information Technology evolution, "data-center convergence." Oddly the technology companies that are working on it are typically communicating a message about technology, which is expected and has some merit. But really, it just amplifies part of what the larger problem in IT has been in the open systems space from the beginning.

IT is there to serve the goals and objectives of the business. Business leaders care about competitive advantage in top line growth, bottom line efficiency, and risk reduction, end of story. In order to meet and constantly improve on these metrics, IT has the responsibility to implement technologies that support the business objectives and goals.

The most valued asset of business is information. The tools that yield the greatest value are their business applications. Business applications are the most visible technology components seen in a company and the ones that are most directly tied to their business and P&L.

This is not new. But changes are happening. The speed, and scale of business is expanding at an unprecedented velocity, straining IT systems beyond what they are capable of when using old approaches. The web has extended the reach of potential customers, users expect instant on mobility from anywhere, and all of this and other things have created an explosion of data to store and process. Evolving the architectural infrastructure to manage and meet these demands is what convergence is all about.

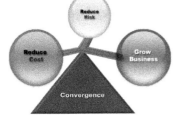

The data center convergence strategy will emerge as the largest change to Information Technology in the history of IT with profound impact to the human experience.

Convergence sets the stage for a globally cooperative set of computing resources tackling computationally intensive tasks and services that are but dreams today. A high performance world of solutions through rich new sources of information, connection, mobility, security, and discovery accelerated exponentially.

The end vision is awe-inspiring, the direction is now logically building, and it will happen. But really, the evolutionary strategy bridging us to data-center convergence (a.k.a. The Software Defined Data Center as well as the Vblock Infrastructure Platform) is a massive refinement to a strategic direction that came from a similar set of goals from a very long time ago.

The goal has always been to get more done, with less. Less capital expense for buying things[1], less operating expense to manage and run things, and less risk to the business. Among other things, these objectives have resulted in massive adoption rates of virtualization and consolidation.

The difference is, now we want to take IT structure and services to a global scale, the velocity of data will be like nothing we have ever seen before which by today's standards is amazingly small compared to the coming data tsunami. Adding to the abundant amount of traffic already flowing through the Internet is the rapidly building tsunami known as the Internet of Things (IoT).

The IoT are device like sensors and actuators that are embedded in physical objects. They are already being deployed everywhere, from roadways to pacemakers, some are linked through wired connections and others and wireless networks.

New wireless standards to accommodate IOT wirelessly are emerging such as 802.15.4e with low power consumption rates allowing devices to run for years at lower bandwidth levels than typical Wi-Fi.

---

[1] The server business continued to slide in the second quarter with worldwide revenue and unit sales down, IDC said in August 2013. The slowing demand is a combination of factors including consolidation, virtualization, and migration initiatives by mainstream small and medium businesses and enterprise customers, and dampening demand for new IT projects in difficult economic conditions.

IoT devices will often be using the same Internet Protocol (IP) that connects the Internet. These networks are expected to churn out huge volumes of data that will flow to computers for real time analysis. This is the root of what people are calling Big Data. Why is this happening? When these smart sensors can both sense the environment and communicate, they become tools for understanding complexity and responding to it swiftly.

For instance, in high winds, what if an IoT sensor could have detected a high power transmission line had broken, and before it started a forest fire, it could have automatically shut the power down to that part of the grid. These physical information systems are now beginning to be deployed, and some of them even work largely without human intervention.

The amount of infrastructure needed to make real-time decisions for this high velocity data today, and especially into the future is gigantic. Architecturally, centrally controlled, policy based management, network security for mobility, the development of universal query languages for unstructured and semi-structured data for real time streaming analysis, are among the challenges vigorously under development.

Put mildly, lots of invention will be needed and is underway now.

Even with all of the development challenges, data center convergence will emerge as virtualization continues to expand in servers, storage and networks, centralized management will scale to match, and analytics can take advantage of unstructured, semi-structured, and real-time streaming data to tame and extract new and emerging value out of the vast deluge of data, including the arrival of device and sensory data.

The Value of Convergence

Converged, or software defined data centers and systems, promise the ability to deal with this tremendous scale, while not allowing capital asset utilization to falter.

The fruition of <u>convergence</u> provides a way to manage the environment without having the old level of complexity and human involvement in scaling to meet the rapidly changing demands of business. Ultimately convergence allows a Line of Business manager to expect tremendous flexibility and agility to quickly, and optimally take advantage of emerging business trends or to react to immediate changes and opportunities, or even newly emerging needs.

At a high level, converged systems create an environment that can define a virtual environment to the end user or application while automatically managing and optimizing the physical resources in the data center to align with business objectives.

The linkage between needs of the user and the required infrastructure, the discovery of real assets, the optimization of the configuration and utilization and the assets on a hyper-scale is provided by the vision of converged systems.

Getting Started

As the Chinese philosopher Lao-tzu once said around 550 B.C., "A journey of a thousand miles begins with a single step." If that is the measure, then we are well underway, with the immediate area of prioritization for achieving the converged data center focused on expanding the adoption and management through broad scale virtualization of servers, storage and networks.

Vitalization and networks are the on-ramp to clouds, which are expanding both internally and externally. With these and other converged infrastructure building blocks properly in place; data mobility will be enabled far beyond current limitations. Along with user abilities to have a mobile office with permissions that follow them, many devices will join the current and IoT network, reporting the status of everything one can imagine. In addition to mobility, a whole new class of business inspired decision support will emerge through cataloging and analyzing streaming data used to gain business advantage.

This brave new world adds up to exponential growth of everything in the infrastructure, servers, storage networks, and all of the software needed to make it work. Leading businesses that adopt converged infrastructures and the analytics derived from Big Data will outperform their competitors by 20% in financial metrics[2].

---

[2] Source: Gartner

The Fatal Flaw

While this is the grand vision and centerpiece of industry

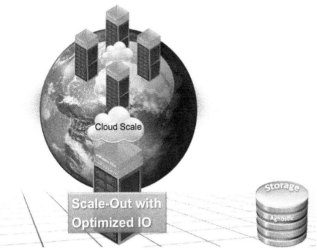

leaders, analysts conversations and marketing organizations globally, there is a fatal flaw that seems to be invisible and unfavorably ignored that distils down to one mitigating technology centered problem - economics.

All of the above vision depends on virtualization, which by its very nature has created a show stopping, and unresolved issue. The issue; cramming the work load of many standalone servers down a constricted physical storage path, retards performance beyond what is acceptable to users, and beyond what is acceptable for business leaders to pay to solve the issue through over spending in infrastructure.

Specifically, you can buy your way out of the issues, which the vendor community would love, but the return value of the technology gorged solution for your business, can't justify the expense to get there.

How can we move to a brave new converged world, with problems that mitigate an economically viable infrastructure? Has the fatal flaw of performance through virtualization, and the associated costs to store unimaginably large amounts of data been solved?

Unfortunately, no. Not at least as a single solution. Like so much of the rest of the open-systems world, there are pieces that are available from different suppliers. The individual pieces serves to address individual problems. But if you look at the IO architecture as a whole, there is no single solution available.

IABPro is working to promote architectural changes in the IO layer, which would solve the issue. These changes need to be a fundamental part of an integration of both hardware and various layers of software.

This paper will layout the fundamental issues, as well as a proposal for changes that need to be made in order for convergence to become a economically pleasing reality.

Getting to Convergence

This paper is not intended to cover the many architectural considerations of technologies that are emerging that will eventually deliver on the strategy of convergence.

Instead, we will take a deep architectural and technological look at areas that are crucial to the success of convergence. Specifically the IO architecture.

With convergence, we have arrived at a crossroads of objectives. Down one path is a break-down stopping not only today's growth but also the future through performance congestion, and untenable storage costs.

The other road is convergence solution enabling, with an IO architectural break-though and pivotal technology development, at the right time and place.

To better understand the power of a new IO architecture for the convergence solution, we need to understand the nature, context and challenges of the current state of the IO architecture, and it's many limitations.

Step One - Virtualize

As a starting point for achieving the convergence vision, the big developmental challenges for convergence, is in resources that are not centrally managed, utilized well, and are increasingly too complex to secure and manage.

Ironically, virtualization, a key technology designed for effective use of resources, is in many ways the heart of the entire breakdown going forward.

Virtualization is not new; it remains central to our future, yet it is not virtualization software alone that will allow the full fruition of achieving an efficient converged infrastructure.

Far from it, virtualization is only a single layer in a much more complex stack that is required to deliver convergence. Some of the layers already exist and are functional today, while others are vigorously under development.

In the Beginning

It may surprise you, but virtualization has been around for

1960-1980s	1990-2012	2013-Beyond
Mainframes	**Client Server**	**Cloud**

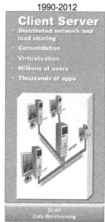

a long while. From the days of mainframes, the Amdahl 470 V/8, first shipped in 1980, incorporated the first real hardware based virtualization known as "Multiple Domain Facility" (MDF). IBM Mainframes had a software-based approach called Logical Partitioning (LPAR).

Both helped to improve the utilization of processor resources, and ultimately saved money. However, mainframes had other management software known as DFSMS built into the IBM operating systems that did, and still does manage resources quit effectively, efficiently, and securely. This can be thought of as stack management because the management resources are consolidated into processing resources.

The Rise of Client-Servers

But as the world transitioned from centrally managed mainframes to distributed client-server systems, no single stack managed solution (i.e., mainframes) emerged as either effective or the de-facto standard. Instead, literally hundreds of specialized pieces of software were developed to run at the server level as niche market plays, all to provide some individual management capability similar is some small way to what was an integrated management stack in the IBM mainframe.

Lots of individual pieces were created, with none of them working together very well, and are therefore all more or less each standalone. As a result, even more storage resources are underutilized. This is the point that caused storage to undertake a transformation with management software increasingly being built into the array.

Nevertheless in the mid 90's, applications moving to client-server systems were stampeding away from the raised floor data-centers to become individually controlled departmental servers. With no real consolidation of management or security in the stack, the alleged capital savings that sparked client-server growth in the first place, turned into an operating expense and risk related economic disaster.

Oddly, that stimulated the reinvention and expansion of virtualization, learned from the experience in mainframes and now targeted at the client-server world.

But a more integrated method of centrally managing resources efficiently was still missing, and as client-server virtualization grew, so did performance-choking bottlenecks to storage.

In addition, with storage management increasingly deployed in arrays, management of servers and arrays was increasingly siloed.

Virtualization Rises – Consolidation Underway

As viable virtualization technologies emerged for the client-server environment, the next big push was to get all the servers that were located in departmental closets, back into the glass-house, and virtualize all of it. We called that consolidation.

Yet, even today, with infrastructure back in the glass-house, according to the 451 Group, less than a third of data centers that have been surveyed believe their infrastructure is sufficiently virtualized.

That translates to inefficiencies that are costly. To that end, virtualization remains a primary objective through 2015 or beyond, limiting IT department's attention to switch to other initiatives including convergence, until it is done.

So as of 2013[3] while everyone is aware of the performance problems and follow-on storage gluttony server virtualization creates, overall servers are about 51% virtualized, but the number of organizations dealing with virtualized production applications has doubled over last year.

The Management Challenge

What we didn't expect was how difficult it was going to be to manage everything as the enormous collapsing physical infrastructure moved back into the virtualized data-center.

The angst was only made worse, when a company acquired another, and all of the options of open standards that one architecture team implemented, were completely different than the other and by the way, also incompatible.

In many cases it caused people to have to start from scratch to have a common set of standards they would follow. This is just one of many management issues.

Perhaps reducing the variables is one of the drivers that are causing the migration off of RISC architectures and onto x86 as the standard platform. It is now estimated that 80% of all workloads are running on x86 with only 13% now on RISC.

---

[3] Source: 451 Group Server and Virtualization Study.

With all of the attention and work on server virtualization underway, nobody anticipated the management and performance issues in storage.

Virtualized Storage Capacity – Largely Wasted

There are a number of factors driving storage cost overruns.

1. Mismanaged capacity
2. Data duplication
3. Excessive capacity purchased to meet performance objectives

While significant capacity is lost from mismanagement, most of the conversation about wasted capacity typically centers on data that is duplicated[4].

Making matters worse, data growth has accelerated, in fact emerging communications technologies matched to rich content has maintained exponential growth rates. 40% to 50% compounded growth rates are common.

---

[4] Allocated but not used, and Orphaned data contribute to large amounts of waste as well

Duplication from Backups

In the clustered and grid computing environments, as well as the results caused by consolidation and virtualization, it is an unfortunate reality to find data to be highly redundant.

There is a built in efficiency paradox. From a protection architecture point of view, IT administrators purposely replicate data as a part of their protection strategy and architecture.

Data replication insures high levels of availability, and is accomplished though various techniques such as point in time copies, continuous data protection, snapshots, mirrors, etc. Backup applications save these copies.

Active Data Duplication

From an active data point of view, data can be replicated for repurposing to be used in data mining and other business processes.

Another attribute of data replication is plain old file sharing. Some of it is ad hoc as might be found from email, while some of it can be semi-structured as can be found in SharePoint. It may also just be load sharing.

Replicated Data Mounts

Depending on usage examples, replicated data can range from a few copies of a file to thousands. Backup applications save and replicate these as well. No one would argue that protection is vital, but the result of data protection is mass duplication. 15 to 20 copies of everything are not unusual on disk, and are even greater when tape is involved.

However, beyond even replication today, lots of storage capacity is still mismanaged and wasted, virtualizing that, just makes it harder to find causing even more waste.

Exacerbating the waste issue, storage vendors built storage management tools into the arrays, with only pockets of complete storage management capabilities remaining in the stack that could look across the whole storage infrastructure.

Mismanaged Capacity

Most servers and storage infrastructure still follow a siloed mentality, using array-based management. This results in no central way of managing all of the resources for capacity efficiency or performance objectives, as workloads wax and wane. At least not efficiently.

For performance yes, there are capabilities such as vMotion for storage tiering, but even that has the potential of major performance penalties to an already saturated storage backend. More on this later.

From an efficiency point of view, mainframes have had efficient capabilities from the beginning. The cost of not centrally managing storage as mainframes have done in the client-server world has been costly.

Many studies have commonly shown as much as 70% of storage capacity is mis-utilized and could be returned to free-pool.

This frequently is the equivalent of millions of dollars of loss or storage overspending. Some tools like Symantec's Veritas™ products when used to meet their potential, improve utilization efficiency greatly.

Virtualized Storage Performance – Another Major Issue

Current virtualization does strive to balance performance objectives by dynamically moving workloads to servers that have the appropriate amount of performance available. All well and good from a processing power point of view. Where this falls apart is when the server must reach down to talk to the storage. Commonly with up to 20 times greater amounts of IO demand on an IO path as compared to what was there prior to virtualization[5] and consolidation. The IO path freeway is as jammed as California's 405 at peak load (which is nearly always).

Of course this means nobody is going anywhere very fast, and it is aggravating. The server virtualization folks coded up a solution for that. They would migrate storage volumes to higher performing storage tiers when you need to go real fast.

---

[5] A reasonable estimation is that four single CPU VMs can be supported per CPU core. However, this will vary by as little as 1-2 per core, and up to 8-10 per core, based on the average CPU utilization of applications running on VMs

That approach is like saying, "I'm sorry the freeway is jammed, here try this Ferrari." Sorry, the freeway is still jammed; in this case at the server level, therefore – migrating the volume in the same IO path had no benefit.

You need faster performance, which is really just low latency, but you also you need less traffic for even that to work.

The IO Brick Wall

Again, the major issue in storage, after virtualizing, is that fewer physical servers are supporting more virtualized servers across the same number of IO paths, resulting in IO bottlenecking performance issues.

Virtualizing as fast as Rabbits

The practice of consolidation did slow down the sprawl of real hardware and software resources used to support a single application. However, because we started virtualizing them; the problem of managing increasing numbers of servers in fact has become worse.

Virtualization software makes it easy to clone up new environments with a simple snapshot. So what was once known as IT sprawl of individual silos of physical resources, has now become VM sprawl of logical resources[6]. Different day, far worse problem. On one hand, virtualization has reduced the number of required servers.

On the other hand, VM sprawl has lead to unexpected growth in the number of virtual machines implemented and the inherent mushrooming demand that places on IO.

Fewer physical servers supporting an increasing ratio of virtual servers, has placed enormous strain on the amount of storage IO ports a server is typically limited to, the interconnect, and finally the amount of storage ports available with their limitations of bandwidth and throughput.

---

[6] The number of virtual and physical servers (mostly virtual) will grow tenfold over the next 10 years. The amount of information generated will increase by a factor of 50. And the number of files a data center must manage will grow by a factor of 75, or more says IDC. Globally, in an IDC survey, respondents report server virtualization and server consolidation as their top IT objectives during the next year, and in many cases their physical infrastructure is preventing this growth. Nearly three-quarters of the respondents from each region cite server virtualization as their most important initiative.

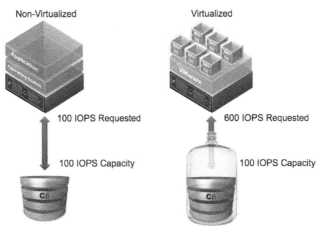

Again, the IO that used to be spread across maybe 20 physical servers and the amount of aggregated ports they had (i.e. 80), once virtualized, is now funneled down to the same work as 20 servers, that are now virtual servers, and exist on one physical IO suffocating server (4 ports typically).

That's bottlenecking and it amplifies the fact that while server performance has enjoyed huge growth, storage has just not kept the same performance growth rate.

The impact is that organizations have had to purchase additional servers to reduce the ratio and storage hardware to fight these IO bottlenecks by trying to spread the IO load across more storage devices as they get choked.

Often the gains of virtualizing the server are that IT departments have simply traded server savings for storage costs. Unless the industry addresses this IO challenge, users cannot cost effectively realize the full potential of their current and growing virtual environment, and they may as well forget a converged data center of the future. The economics are crushing.

Defining the IO Performance Gap

In a recent IDG survey, nearly 80% of all respondents report their companies are planning changes to their physical infrastructure during the next 12 months. That's because, as cited by 80% of all respondents, physical infrastructure challenges are inhibiting the progress of important data center objectives, with virtualization as a primary goal.

As the client virtualizes their assets, the IO performance gap will become the major contributor to this problem, which is plaguing all high-density compute and storage environments, which is the inevitable outcome of a virtualized data center today, and significantly gets worse under the load of the future's converged data center.

Specifically, the IO performance gap is a measure of how much the performance of processors has grown, versus the rather paltry amount of performance gains we have seen in storage throughput (how fast data is moved) and Input/Output oPerations per Second (IOPS) or how fast and how many times you can access a disk in a second.

There is perpetual misunderstanding on this point, so let's clarify it.

Moore's law relates to the observation that predicts, over the history of computing hardware, the number of transistors on integrated circuits doubles approximately every two years, at least so far. That prediction will come to an end around 2020, because semi-conductor manufactures don't think they can make circuits on silicon as small as a nanometer (carbon nanotubes may be the answer however).

The confusion is this. Just because transistor density doubles, it doesn't necessarily follow that the performance of the processor, measured in Millions of Instructions Per Second (MIPS) executed, also doubles. So to use the growth of transistors as a base line of performance gain is inaccurate.

However, here are some numbers that are clear:

Performance Since 1986:

1. CPU performance (MIPS) has had a 44% CAGR (a major driver to multi-core processors and multi-threading)

2. Storage throughput performance has only advanced at 20% CAGR in the last 27 years (how fast data comes off the disk)

3. IO Bus performance has advanced at 27% in the same period (how fast data moves across a storage network)

4. Storage density has advanced at a 61% CAGR (how much capacity a HDD has)

5. However, as storage density increases, access demand rates to that disk also increases, creating contention, which creates wait time, which slows performance. This is known as an access density issue and is measured as the number of IOs served per Gigabyte

Of course there are more dramatic ways of looking at this.

1. CPU growth has grown from (1986) an Intel 386 capable of 9.9 MIPS to a processor called Sandy-Bridge (2013) which is capable of 177,730 MIPS signifying a performance increase multiple of **17,953 times**. Not bad.

2. In 1986 the HDD IO Bus was IDE and it was good for about 2 MegaBytes a second, today there is Fiber Channel over Ethernet which runs at 10 gigabits of 1.25 Gigabytes per second, or an increase of **600 times.**

3. A 3.5' HDD in 1983 had a capacity of 10 MegaBytes, today you can buy a 3.5' with 4 TeraBytes an increase of **400,000 times**.

4. Because HDD spin rates and disk arm armatures really haven't changed significantly – IOPs rates

are about 10 times better in that period of time.
(1986 - ST506 - 3,600 RPM – 85ms Latency)

In some ways, these numbers don't look that bad, but in reality the impact is horrible and getting worse.

Understanding Storage Performance

The limitations of performance from a server point of view are a combination of:

1. Processor workload
2. Processing power
3. Memory size
4. Memory Speed
5. Throughput
6. Input Output (IO) demand out to storage
7. The amount of available paths to storage
   a. Both from the server and how many ports are available on the storage controller

Also consider how busy the servers are alone (without other conflicting server traffic) as well as with other servers creating IO traffic contention, what type of interconnect mesh is used, the amount of cache[7], block sizes, random versus sequential IO patterns, the ratio of reads to writes, the speed of the disk array controller, the RAID level used, how many hard disk drives are used in the RAID stripe to spread the IO across, and the type of hard disk used along with latency[8] characteristics.

---

[7] Low cache hit percentages typically will drive up response times. A cache miss requires IO access to backend storage. Low cache hit percentages also tend to increase the utilization percentage of the backend storage because of the incremental backend IO needed to refresh the cache, which will also adversely affect the backend throughput and response times.
High write-cache delay percentages will drive up the write response times.

There are also considerations for the impact of cache in an array, or the use of non-centrally attached arrays technology, like server side persistent storage. We will purposely ignore that because it adds even more complexity for trying to understand the fundamentals.

Let's use an example. We will assume that a single server with all of its virtual machines can generate an average of 40,000 IOPS using 4K blocks, which is sufficient to meet user demand.

This will be driven down Host Bus Adapters (HBA) through any of four IO paths through an interconnect mesh, such as Fiber Channel, to a storage array.

High transfer block sizes typically indicate more of a streaming type workload, in which case the overall data rates are more important than the IO rates and the response times.

[8] Latency is a measure of the delay from the time data is requested until it is delivered. Factors include servers, workload, memory, caches, and networks. From a storage point of view after an IO is received, it is the sum of the time it takes for the electronics to process RAID and drive commands, time it takes for heads to move to the correct location (seek time), time it takes for the heads to settle, and time it takes for the platter to rotate to the correct location (rotational latency) to read or write a given amount of data. All of these factors throttle the amount of IOPS that are possible.

In architecting a solution for this, it is common to look at the first part of the problem to be solved, but ignore the rest. Here is why, an IT storage architect will need to know how much storage capacity is needed, and what the throughput and IOPs demand rate is. Some people start by only considering the capacity problem, but don't give very much thought to overall performance. They just always try to buy the fastest arrays.

Making matters worse, when they test for performance, they use a test-bed, which erroneously performs adequately for a full production workload - given the limited amount of users in the test. Again, this is partially exacerbated by the fact that many architects believe buying the best is always the safest position, so they tend to buy performance drives.

Often this produces adequate performance for the test, HOWEVER, when it goes to production, performance is often woefully short, everyone is unhappy, which really puts everyone in a pickle.

But, to carry on with the example and show how some of this progresses, in this case if we needed 15 TBs of capacity along with some performance, we could choose to configure this using 15K SAS drives that have a capacity of 600 GBs. If our RAID stripe is spread across 5 drives, then we will need 7 RAID 5 sets and controllers, which will give us 28 useable drives or 15.3 TBs of usable capacity.

Good – the capacity problem is solved, and nobody is upset with the budget.

But what about performance? How many IOPs can I get from this configuration? The answer is partially a dependency of workload and how often an application reads something versus writes something. But if we were to consider an OnLine Transaction Processing (OLTP) system, the read to write ratios can vary from 80/20 reads versus writes to 50/50 R/W. Lets just say we want to target an 80/20 R/W ratio.

This configuration is woefully short of the IOPS needed to support a demand rate of 40,000 IOPS (a common server performance demand rate). Our 28 drives will allow for around 4,522 IOPS given everything above. About 92% short on the amount of drives needed to satisfy our performance objective.

To have adequate performance, we need 85 RAID groups and controllers to satisfy the server performance demand rate. That includes a total of 340 15K 146 GB drives, which will deliver 54,910 frontend IOPS with RAID 5, at a 80/20 R/W ratio. The usable capacity is also more than we need at 45 TBs even though we are now using 146 GB drives instead of 600 GB drives.

The expense to have a storage array configured for capacity and performance means that we had to overbuy capacity, and we had to have 85 RAID 5 controllers and RAID sets to insure the lowest possible latency and IO Wait time in order to hit our performance objective of 40,000 IOPs. We will come back to latency shortly.

RAID Matters

We all know that unlike a PC with one drive, an enterprise will use an array with many drives. A RAID 5 (see the RAID 5 illustration on page 41) array will generally have at least 5 drives, so it's a simple multiplication to figure out the array performance. 5 (15k SAS drives)*190 (IOPS) = 950 IOPs.

Here is the first big caveat, you can get 950 IOPs if you are reading from 5 15K RPM drives in a RAID 5 protection scheme (assuming no caching benefits), however writing is a much different activity.

The Problem with RAID

In storage subsystems, redundancy results from either writing the same data to multiple drives (known as mirroring) a la RAID 1, or writing extra protection data (parity or ECC) across the array a la RAID 5[9].

---

[9] Protection data is calculated so that the failure of one or possibly

RAID 5 stripes data at the block level across all disks in the RAID set or stripe, RAID 5 also distributes and stripes parity across all drives in the RAID set. Parity is distributed on a round robin basis allowing independent reading of different blocks from several drives simultaneously with no
single drive acting as a bottleneck.

The storage capacity of a RAID 5 stripe is equal to N-1 drives because the equivalent capacity of one drive is holding parity data. A single drive failure allows data to continue to be served, albeit in a degraded performance mode.
When the drive is replaced, it can be rebuilt, further impacting performances because of all of the backend IO to both serve and rebuild. Read performance during a drive failure is impacted because the RAID controller has to read the whole strip across multiple drives, including the parity, and then rebuild what the data should be, before satisfying the read request to the server.

Beyond failure conditions, when simply writing data, each RAID 5 write will cause four disk IOs at the backend of the storage array - two reads and two writes:

---

more disks (depending on the RAID type used i.e. RAID 5 versus RAID 6) in the array will not result in loss of data. Subsystems are designed to allow for hot plugging a failed disk with a replacement. The lost data from the failed drive is then reconstructed from the remaining data in a defined RAID set and the associated parity data.

1. First a read for the data that is to be eventually overwritten

2. Second a read for that data's associated parity

    a. Then the RAID controller performs an exclusive-or calculation that includes the old data added to the new data generating the new parity

3. Third we now write the new data back to the RAID Stripe, and

4. Fourth we write the new parity (that we just calculated for the changed stripe)

Frontend IOPS versus Backend IOPS

Frontend IO vs. Backend IO With RAID 5

Frontend IOPs are the total number of read and write operations per second generated by a server and delivered through a Host Bus Adaptor (HBA) into a interconnect mesh, that are serviced through ports on a storage array.

So while the server may see 1 write IO, the backend of the array as explained above, when using RAID 5 had to issue 4 IOs (times five drives or 20 IOs) for each of the frontend IOPs (backend calculations typically ignore the individual drive IO and only count the number of IOs to the stripe). Also, the operation may appear to complete earlier if the file is in cache.

Backend IOPS therefore are the total number of read and write operations per second that a controller inside the storage array can service through RAID stripped storage spread across Hard Disks.

Backend IOPS are highly sensitive to IO that is writing, resulting in variable performance based on the read/write ratio mix and type of RAID being used.

Latency Matters

While IOPs are a good gauge of storage performance, alone it is not enough to understand the dynamics of storage performance. Footnote number 8 details factors to consider when measuring storage performance, all of which aggregate factors affecting IO performance.

Unfortunately, IOPs can be mischievously misrepresented as well, by playing with the numbers that control what IOPs are. When IOPs are being misrepresented, it typically means that disclosure for how their IOPs were derived and hidden.

For instance, are they random or sequential IOPs? What is the block size (probably not realistic, a favorite trick)? What is the ratio of reads to writes? What is the cache hit ratio? What kind of drives were used? For that type of drive, do they really add up to a realistic IOPs performance level? What was the RAID scheme? How many usable RAID drives were part of the calculation? What is the RAID write penalty? Was that factored?

Don't forget the Frames

To be really precise, another layer of consideration in performance planning considers the network mesh, like Fibre Channel and the frame size and rate used to communicate with a storage array.

Again, a deeper conversation than intended for this paper, but suffice it say that because a standard FC Frame only carries a payload of 2K Bytes, the amount of frames chatting across a wire increase as an application increases the transferred block size request.

An 8K IO block needs 4 frames. In this case, 1 IO produces 4 frames transferred in a sequence. Making this worse, 100 IOPs causes 400 Frames being received by the storage frontend and that can produce 400 IOs at the storage backend in a RAID 5 array.

Because of the small payload of the FC frame, when we again think about what used to be 20 physical servers each with four ports, now being funneled down to just one physical server with four ports, you can see that congestion in the mesh is also a consideration for overall performance.

Current switches are able to detect congestion and route to paths that are less busy. But in this case we have a server that only has 4 paths. They can all get busy, and therein lies another problem. Sometimes a SAN will slow down because of a slow draining device. A slow draining device is one that is requesting information faster than it can put it away.

A congested backend storage array is a good example. This can spread as the switch tries to load balance. The ultimate impact is felt in application slowdowns or even time-outs. Reducing the amount of overall traffic is key to solving this, and caching, inline deduplication and compression can do that.

Short Stroking

Partitioning a HDD to a fractional amount of its capacity, say half, has the effect of only using the outside half of a platter. That will reduce the seek latency of a drive by half. If you had an average seek latency of 3.7ms, now it would be 1.85ms (rotational latency remains the same at 2ms). That would take a 15K RPM HDD average response time from 5.71ms to 3.85ms.

So is it faster, yes. Does it solve the bigger problem, no! 3.85ms is still as slow as a slug for high demand IOPs environments.

Fragmented Files – the IO Blender

Inherent behaviors associated with x86 virtual environments cause additional I/O bottlenecks. For example, files written to a general-purpose local disk file system are typically broken into pieces and stored as disparate clusters in the file system. This happens because each virtual server running an operating system must reference it's individual file system.

Because so many virtual machines are all writing, reading, and deleting files, the use of virtual volumes changes from contiguous amounts of storage capacity, to fragmented storage capacity. Meaning if the smallest capacity of the disk drive is 4,096 bytes (4K Block) and you need to write 1 megabyte, you could wind up with something that looks like the table to the right. A total of 49 IOs were issued to find enough space to write a 1 MB file.

IOs	Block Sizes Available	Bytes of Data
1	128,000	128,000
5	64,000	320,000
10	32,000	320,000
5	16,000	80,000
8	8,000	80,000
18	4,000	72,000
Total 49		1,000,000

In a virtualized environment, every virtual machine's virtual disks become fragmented, creating increasingly greater needs for bandwidth and IO capacity to sort out where to put incoming data written to the volume. Each piece of a file requires its own processing cycles to issue the IO – resulting in an unwelcome increase in processor, network and storage overhead.

This extra IO, slows all Virtual Machines on the same server hardware, network, and storage reducing the benefits of virtualization. Shortly we will explore the additive effects of serialized latency.

But for now, this phenomenon is sometimes referred to as the IO blender effect.

Imagine for a moment that you had a new IO architecture that included deduplication, optimized fragmented write, and compression. The deduplication component would reduce the probability of even doing a write by 98%.

If you were so unlucky as to actually have to do the write, then the 50% efficient optimized fragmented write capability could reduce the 49 IOs down to say 25.

If then we were using compression, we might be down to 4 or 5 IOs.

Imagine how much more efficient it would be if instead of our 49 IOs from the example, it could be done in say 4 or 5 IOs!

Multiple this savings by the potential for a IOPs demand rate of 40,000, and now we have reduced the total number of IOs going down the IO architecture by the amount we had added by virtualizing.

An amazing possibility!

External Storage Performance Summary

To finish up on factors that impact latency here is a longer list of things to consider in storage performance.

1. Latency matters – greater amounts of latency (or response time), causes greater amounts of IO wait time, which causes greater amounts of user dissatisfaction.

2. **Major rule:** You can't generate IOPs to a storage array, any faster than a server can request them. Factors:

3. Processor workload

4. Type, number of processors, cores, and speed

5. Amount of DDR3 and speed

6. IO Wait time

7. Interconnect mesh quantity, types, and speeds (framing or stack inefficiencies)

8. The less latency you incur as you move up the storage hierarchy, the more IOPs the storage can sustain –

9. But you can never serve IO faster than the server is requesting it (using a legitimate workload), negating the false value claims of ridiculously high IOPs, i.e., 1 million IOPS

10. Storage arrays performance will peak as their front end and/or back-end saturates. Factors:

11. RAID write penalties

12. RAID read penalties when in degraded mode

13. RAID rebuild time

14. Temporary reads errors, and block relocations

15. Percentage of reads to writes

16. Random IO versus Sequential IO

17. Data hot spots

18. Locality of reference of the data or lack therein

19. Types, capacity, and performance of HDD or SSD used

20. How drives are partitioned, i.e., short stroking

21. Conflicting traffic from data protection tools or other servers

22. An inadequate amount of cache in the array, or inefficient caching algorithms

23. The larger the payload (data), the fewer IOPs, likewise – you can generate and service more IOPs as you decrease the payload

The Impact of Storage Latency

It is difficult to get your mind around the impact of really small amounts of time. So lets normalize this to timeframes we do understand to gain an appreciation for why latency is important.

Beginning with the server, if we stretched the internal clock rate of a CPU from a timeframe measured at 83 billionths of a second, out to a second, and then used that number as a multiple to create a time constant to stretch the IO subsystem time out in the same relative amount, here is what happens.

- A server makes a request for IO to DDR3. That takes 1 second.

- The server makes a request for IO out to SSD, what used to be 200 millionths of a second of latency now takes 4 minutes.

- The server makes a request for IO out to a SAN array, what used to take 10 thousandths of a second of latency now takes 3 hours and 21

m
i
n
u
t
e
s
.

S
e

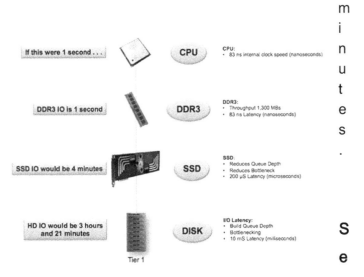

rialization Hangs on Time

Here is why this is such a big problem. Most applications are coded to operate as a single threaded operation. Another way of saying this is that they don't parallelize work queues and spread the work queue across multiple resources (with a some exceptions, like Oracle). Instead, they execute one instruction after another and one IO after another, each has to complete before the next one can proceed.

In the case of storage IO, for this example, this would mean that the operating system issues an instruction to service an application request for IO. It then puts the application on hold, and leaves it on hold, until the request for IO is satisfied by the storage subsystem.

Applications and Users Hang on Time

Using the example above, if that happens to be to a disk

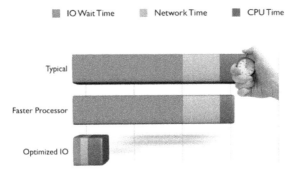

array, the application and all of the users that are using that application, wait for 3 hours and 21 minutes minimum for each IO. If the array happen to be busy with other IO traffic, such is the common case in the IO traffic jams created by virtualization, the wait time can get down right ugly.

IO Through DDR3 in no Time

To contrast that, if the request for IO was made through a shadow volume in server DDR3, the wait time is reduced from 3 hour 21 minutes down to a second. Remember, these are not actual times; they are just stretched out to time frames we can more readily identify with and understand, the relative time ratios are correct. In reality - we are contrasting the difference in 83 nanoseconds to 10 milliseconds. But now you can see why it is such a big deal.

To carry this out a little further, it is not uncommon for a database to request a block of data, wait for the IO request to be satisfied by the storage array, then update it in memory, and then write the block out again, while waiting some more.

If you multiple these process times by hundreds of thousands of transactions, you have a compounding potential for various types of wait related disasters, from databases that can no longer viably operate, users that are very unhappy, maybe trades that can't be performed on a stock exchange, and even the possibility of violating certain legal requirements resulting in monetary penalties.

The Best Latency is No-Latency!

Databases and analytics are particularly sensitive to latency. Databases make several kinds of requests for IO that need to be acknowledged quickly, typically under 10ms, and writes especially in well under 5ms.

Especially critical, redo log[10] writes need to be acknowledged almost instantaneously for a heavy-write oriented database with an expectation for response in under 1ms (caching required).

---

[10] A redo log switch should occur every 15 to 30 minutes as a rule of thumb. Switching too often leads to performance congestion.

If a database can't write to its redo log fast enough for a single write, the database application and all of its users stall until that write can complete, at which point it will move on. However, if the database is constantly delayed in writing to its redo log, the user experience will be constantly unacceptable.

Even in a multi-threaded application like Oracle, latency counts. Oracle can operate IO in synchronous mode, which essentially is the same as a single threaded operation. But even in asynchronous mode, an Oracle database generating about 15,000 IOPs may see 25ms of latency for random IO and only 5ms for sequential.

Yet that is enough for the CPU running that application to see a 90% wait time. This is a sure indicator that the application performance would benefit from lower storage latency even though it is meeting IOPs demand rates.

By the way, because of the possibility of data corruption sensitive data will likely be in synchronous mode anyway, again making the problem even more pronounced.

The Storage Hierarchy

The storage industry has been talking about tiering storage into different cost and performance layers for years to address the latency problem.

In some ways it has backfired. While there are very definite and predictable slopes that show that as data ages, the re-reference probability drops precipitously, you still have to ignore some files like operating systems, applications, and database indices which tend to reside in high performance storage tiers continually.

But data, which is the lion's share quantitatively, have reference patterns that really fall off with small amounts of age.

As an example, the day a data record is created there is a 100% chance of reference. After just three days, the reference probability drops to 50% and at 90 days it is .01%.

Originally people would just buy the best, fastest, and most expensive storage they could, and put everything on it. As world economic pressure forced IT budgets to find ways to get more done with less money, solutions emerged to look at the reference probability of data, and map aging low reference probability data to cheaper, albeit slower forms of storage.

Most of it works well[11], and it is good - until recently.

That hierarchical or tiered form of data management to reduce cost when applied to applications like VDI, Big Data, and analytics has a profound negative impact on performance of applications up in the server.

In other words, the conventional wisdom of putting large cold data files in the slowest performing storage doesn't work for Big Data and streaming analytics. This is great news for storage vendors.

The largest segment of growth appears to need the fastest storage possible.

This is disastrous news for the data center, they won't be able to afford it.

---

[11] There are very few systems that actually migrate data based on reference probability as much as they migrate based on aging. The downside to this is that two chunks of data can have the same creation date, one is red hot from a reference point of view, while the other is stone cold or dead. Manually figuring this out and migrating defeats the point of automation in tiered storage.

Additionally, the conundrum the industry is facing is that the conventional approach of migrating data up and down storage

> The conundrum the industry is facing is that the conventional approach of migrating data up and down storage tiers typical takes too long, and it saturates storage array performance that is already underwater because of virtualization.

tiers typical takes too long, and it saturates storage array performance that is already underwater because of virtualization while it is migrating.

The solution mentality that is currently being followed it to spread the load across an unaffordable quantity of Tier 1 disk (like 15K SAS), or try to put high hit rate, or hot data all on flash.

The Achilles heel of this strategy is that either approach completely wipes out budgets and still doesn't cover all that needs to be stored in high performance storage.

This brings us full circle back to the original issue; we have an IO performance gap that is a blockade to reaching the goals of a virtualized and converged IT infrastructure and realizing all of the goodness that can produce. Insanity: *"doing the same thing over and over again and expecting different results" - Albert Einstein.*

A new approach is in order.

Mapping Application Tiers to Storage Tiers

Application Tier 3 (as shown in the following graphic) which to date has represented some 25% of the world's information used to easily and appropriately mapped to capacity disk.

But when we add Big Data, some of that tier may need to be all the way up and into Flash to meet streaming analytical objectives.

Using IDC's The Digital Universe as a reference, that means in 2013 where there is thought to be 4 Zettabytes of stored capacity, to meet the performance demand rate some potion (depending on hit ratios) of 1 Zettabytes would need to be stored in Flash and or spread across enough Tier 1 performance disk.

It is just not feasible to cost effectively do this today or into the foreseeable future, and we are headed toward a future in just 7 years where this amount grows by 10 times.

By now you should be able to really feel the urgency for an IO Architecture that can solve these fundamental issues.

Not all data has equal value, nor does data maintain value equally over time

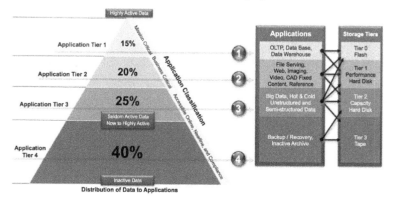

Distribution of Data to Applications

Convergence is a Strategy - Missing an IO Solution

While Business leaders are focused on top-line growth, cost reductions, and mitigating risk, IT is in the midst of an epic transformational change to support these goals.

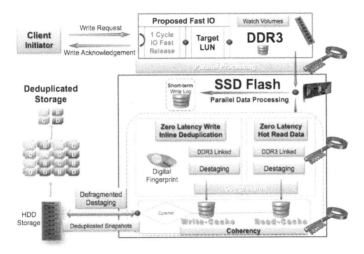

Convergence is the next big thing in IT, but remember - convergence, the software defined data center or Vblock, is a strategy, it is not a product.

The convergence strategy is a method or plan developed to bring about a desired future for a global change in flexible infrastructure connectivity, management, and its overall useful efficiency.

The first challenge is in the development of appropriate architectural vision. It is clear that has been mostly done. Current efforts are in the tactics and activities meant to deal with the development, implementation and testing of foundation technologies, and of course to move from one milestone to another in pursuit of the overall goals.

Convergence is the biggest strategy ever attempted to bridge the skills gap between business minds and organizations of the technology minds in IT.

While businesses leadership certainly has all of the business and financial skills necessary to run and manage a business, they do not have detailed technology skills necessary to create and run a data center. That, of course, is understandable.

Likewise, technology people have plenty of technology skills, but typically lack the same level of acumen in the world of business and finance.

It should not come as a surprise, therefore, to realize that decisions that are made by technology people are often based on the best and sometimes "coolest" technology solution – maybe even the very best technology solution – which is, of course, costly and likely not in alignment with business economic goals.

Herein lies a major goal. It is the objective of the converged infrastructure to change this. Specifically it has been a vision for sometime to use autonomic computing as defined by IBM to simply use business policies that would translate into service level objectives autonomically executed by the data center to meet the business objective.

While convergence is not expected to be quite that level of implementation, it nevertheless is building a foundation from which autonomic computing becomes a real possibility somewhere beyond convergence.

But back to the here and now, problems remain in the implementation of even convergence.

The historically observable and measurable impact to these IO related challenges described earlier, ultimately manifests itself to the business as unacceptable performance with unhappy users and insurmountable expense. It is part of the business to IT paradox. A budget restrictive environment prevents lavish spending, but also limits enough infrastructures to deliver the support of desired business objectives.

These problems are at odds with business leaders, whose objective is to reduce spending, while deriving greater value from IT, which will grow business.

IT is a complex task, and so is running a business. The opportunity is to focus on bridging the gap between the needs and objectives of the business, by assisting in the efficient delivery of IT services.

Convergence is the strategy intended to get us there.

On the other hand, while there is no doubt that managing the converged infrastructure will make the operations staff more productive and improve business economics if done properly, not everybody will happily follow this idea.

Internal Resistance Expected

From a technological point of view, the first challenge most IT operations staff will have is that they are already too resource constrained to manage what they currently have, let alone all of the projected growth. Fancy new architectures and implementation planning to them is work they don't have time for and are nervous to attempt.

They often feel that <u>any</u> change is tantamount to adding additional complexity and therefore risk to the mission critical environments, and that has the potential to bear serious operational impact, which will therefore cause them to push back on any recommended changes. Again, this is rooted by the fear that the introduction of any new technology will only add to their problems and possibly even their own job security.

To be clear, even if a vendor can prove that a solution is technologically superior, the IT technical teams typically still won't want to implement it, unless it seems to be safe because it is supported by the management team. This is a way to manage their risk.

The problem with this potential stalemate is that not moving to the correct technologies may have a serious business cost potentially damaging a businesses' ability to compete.

In defense of the technology teams, if implementation of new technology is done with a parochial mentality, often they are right.

One thing it makes crystal clear, solutions have to be simple to implement, easy to manage, and have solid reliability.

They also must garner the support of business leaders, which means a business justification plan for convergence is mandatory.

Convergence - Getting to Efficiency

DOING THE RIGHT THINGS

The solution to this technology/human dilemma is found in doing the right things, beyond the business plan, one must carefully and methodically create a high performance and optimized infrastructure. Doing the right things is dependent not only on good technology, but also a deep understanding of the operational characteristics of the environment, business processes and application deployments across business applications and infrastructure.

With these things in mind, some good tools, some practical experience, and maybe even some consulting services, one can architect a solution even in the already crowded convergence space that will realistically reduce operational complexity, and improve performance, ultimately reducing operating and capital expenses.

It is sort of a forest and trees challenge. Compounded by the lack of resources in a fast paced and growing environment, once the general architecture of a converged IT infrastructure is implemented – correctly or not, seldom will people go back and question the architecture or the expense versus value it creates.

Even when new applications or in this case architectures are being designed, people tend to implement them the same old way, because it feels less risky. It is the devil you know.

The net impact is that often the benefits of an aging architecture and infrastructure are no longer efficiently delivering peak value to the business. It is no surprise considering that many businesses are growing, and that, of course, has a direct impact on the load and growth placed on the IT infrastructure and the people that manage them.

There is always a shortage of qualified people, which is what leads to this paradox. Without an efficiently converged infrastructure, people will simply continue to buy and use more capacity as a way of dealing with the burgeoning overload rather than efficiently managing what they have.

It is a bit like the warehouse in the Indiana Jones movies. It is cavernous, with plenty of room to add new stuff. It is, of course, much easier to add new things to endless space, than to manage all things inside.

What belongs? What doesn't? It is located in the right place? Is it secure? Is it protected? Are there more than one of the same thing? Should you get rid of the copy? When? How? Does it perform adequately? Does it serve all defined needs?

With an inefficient type of solution, slowly all people realize the infrastructure is strained, as the business has grown beyond the abilities to efficiently deliver IT services from what was originally conceived and implemented.

That's where things get exciting. With the lack of improved insights on how to manage the infrastructure, and with the lack of enough resources to manage the complete environment, the strained technology staff is forced to adopt a "plug the dike" strategy for the growth of the infrastructure, in an attempt to keep the business applications running at expected service levels.

MORE CAPACITY IS NOT THE ANSWER

This is a wonderful opportunity for self-serving vendors to over-sell capacity. Even that is understandable.

If servers and storage were free of cost, one way to approach the issue is to hide the complexity of managing resources behind vast amounts of capacity. However, not only is this expensive from a CAPEX point of view, from an OPEX point of view it is an economic disaster.

Instead of a methodical analysis of how the infrastructure is tied to the needs of the business, and mostly because of industry hype, the effort is most frequently focused on virtualizing and consolidating all servers and storage, without specific regard to optimizing performance up the stack, and efficient management of storage for things such as primary data replication, backup, migration, archive, and tiers of storage for gaining value of data at the right performance levels.

All of these things must be considered, however in the implementation phase, efforts without the right tools and architectural approach have proven to be inefficient and costly.

Convergence Alone is not Enough

Assuredly, the convergence strategy is correct. The time has come to virtualize all resources, managing them from a central location, and spread their power across clouds. The time has come to seamlessly collect all of the data that Internet things can collect and analyze them for improved business value.

It is Time for a New IO Architecture

The time has also arrived to face a show-stopping element that can prevent this vision from being realized.

The conundrum we face is that the growth of data, and the performance of data cannot scale cost effectively using old technology and architectural approaches.

Needed is the ability to deliver an IO layered solution, which is purpose built and priced to accelerate and optimize the converged stack, without adding complexity. We have come to know that the most elegant solutions are so skillfully implemented that they more or less disappear and are never seen.

Observable are the remaining benefits and enabling capabilities that appear as things that just work in ways that satisfy. Simplicity, functionality, performance, and savings are measures of the best technologies.

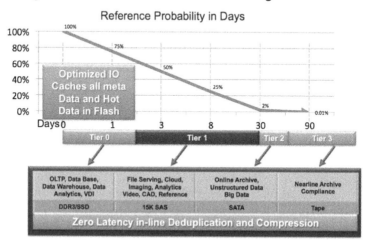

IABPro's proposed architecture proposes the converged infrastructure stack with no new external hardware, it would provide unparalleled levels of performance of highly dynamic tiers of storage without necessarily migrating volumes in the storage arrays.

It could reduce total storage capacity everywhere by as much as 98% with no required management.

It would remove the amount of IO traffic to pre-virtualization levels! It would allow snap-shot copies from one hundredth the amount of space typically required in other technologies. It has the type of management foundation you need, and appears as built-in, such as VAAI compliance. It retains cache coherency for multi-system scale up converged infrastructures.

A New IO Architecture – New Game, New Rules

A new IO architecture isn't a nice to have, it is a must have, and implemented properly will change the rules and barriers we have been constrained to.

A New IO Architecture is the Solution

Hopefully it clear to you that the old approach for serving the scale and volume of the coming IO tsunami is a non-viable option. What is needed is the integration of some technologies that currently individually exist. Unfortunately they don't exist as an integrated solution under one product name.

If they did, we would think of them as a new IO architecture. Lets explore this as if it was a single product, which we will call the New IO Architecture. If we all understand and agree that this, or anything that effectively addresses the problem, as what is needed, perhaps one of the capable vendors will rise to the occasion and integrate these parts.

There are always multiple ways of getting to an end objective. Whatever the end solution is, it must have the ability to integrate, scale, reduce cost, and simplify management.

In the vacuum no other solution, we have given some thought to how to solve the problem using technologies that are available in some form. Again, an effort needs to be established that brings these solutions together.

With that in mind, here is how we have looked at it.

The new IO architecture is an approach uniquely positioned to solve the performance, and capacity conundrum of the converged infrastructure without comprising cost, performance or user satisfaction - in fact, quite the opposite, it should enhances it!

This architectural proposal would yield a breakthrough solution that would be a game changer for the converged infrastructure addressing application challenges associated with virtualization, consolidation, and VDI, with focus on data warehousing, business intelligence, Big Data (using relational & non-relational databases), and the emerging real-time analytic processing of stream computing.

Most of the new IO architecture technology exists today as individual non-integrated parts. These solutions exist and fit in the stack, install in minutes, collectively and individually are a breeze to manage, scales-out to manage zettabytes of storage, and yields big benefits; at least architecturally.

Some of the technologies are unproven even though the approach seems to be right. IABPro's view of a new IO architecture proposes broad scale adoption as a stack layer software solution, although it could be implemented as an onboard hardware offload engine in the future.

Collectively, they would solve the IO performance gap issue, while reducing the amount of storage needed by up to 98%, and would provide an affordable scale-out solution capable of scaling at the rate a converged data center universe expands.

Understanding the New IO Architecture

Technology Description

The new IO architecture is targeted for the converged infrastructure stack and starts with a zero latency inline deduplication capability, via parallel processing. Another key element would include a coherent cache capable of optimized highly defragmented writes, and compression. Coherent hot read caching is also a must in system memory.

Cache Coherency

Cache coherency must exist not only within a single system but, among multiple systems locally, at a minimum to start.
The objectives of virtualized application within the same physical server likely necessitate sharing certain data among multiple Virtual Systems. Various applications do this such as email, Office, SharePoint, databases, and even more sophisticated apps with backend databases like ERPs.

This is a really complex problem. It is being worked on by many companies and really for open systems has not been satisfactorily solved in a way that is in alignment with the ultimate goals of convergence.

Cache coherency begs the question as to whether it should be implemented via hardware with hardware assists, or in the file system. The Lustre file system is viable and a great example of a scaling file system that has a distributed lock manager that works and is high performance. But not everyone wants to be forced into a single file system. People always want the flexibility of choosing whatever file system they prefer, which is why it would be terrific if a viable distributed cache coherency scheme could be built as a hardware assist.

Design and implementation at the hardware level is really complex. Yet here again this is not a new problem. IBM solved this same issue in mainframes with a combination of hardware and OS software. The hardware feature is known as Parallel Sysplex and was supported by the operating system known as MVS/ESA in 1990. It provided for as many as 32 systems to share data coherently.

Later IBM introduced Geographically Dispersed Parallel Sysplex (GDPS), which allow synchronous data mirroring (PPRC) at up to 120 miles (200 km) apart. For distance beyond that IBM introduced GDPS Extended Remote Copy (XRC), which has no distance restrictions for recovery to a remote site. There are other components along the same lines available.

These are examples of both hardware and software approaches to the coherency problem.

It is certain that a hardware level solution is a key technology that must evolve allowing for a fast release between a client initiator and SCSI target if we are to have the perfect solution for the formidable challenges of IO performance and efficient capacity requirements of the converged infrastructure.

Efficient coherent caching and more importantly shared coherent caching is the key to being able to issue an IO that has a fast release. Without a fast release, we have all of the latency issues we suffer from today. Those issues are the key debilitating factors that cause the performance IO gap, and cost overruns.

However, with so many companies working on it, a solution will emerge. This is not a new problem, and as mentioned, it has been solved in the mainframe world with architectures such as Parallel Sysplex allowing multiple mainframes to behave as a single system image. Now is the time for some of the hardware vendors to begin working on a hardware approach that coordinates with various hypervisor suppliers.

When solved, the breakthrough performance benefit is accelerated IO, applications and operating systems benefit all the way up to the top of the stack. The problem of latency disappears as the IO technology makes SSD flash storage behave at the same performance level as DDR3 memory.

Combining this performance ability with a scalable inline multi-threaded parallel processing capability for deduplication, allows for more than one benefit. The first and most obvious is that all storage passing through the new IO architecture layer is now fast and optimized.

As a result, storage capacity requirements are reduced by as much as 98%. Since all things going through the new IO architecture layer are deduplicated, the new IO architecture deduplication engine maintains a copy of meta data, and automatically maintains all data, read and write, which has a high reference probability in SSD flash in cache.

With a multitude of benefits, this results in any high demand rate data automatically migrating up to flash. Once there, and because of the new IO architectures' unique performance capability, any write IO directed to data in SSD flash, will perform at the same performance level as DDR3, essentially no latency whatsoever.

Zero Latency

Let's examine why. When an operating system puts a block of data in flight with a write request through an iSCSI initiator, a related target receives the write request. In the case of the new IO architecture, that iSCSI target exists inside of DDR3 Memory.

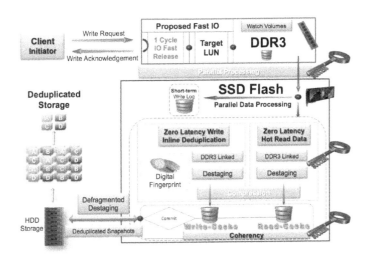

The target stores the write into a memory cache and for safety, immediately stores it to a write log located on SSD for backup. Simultaneously, with the data in flight to the SSD write log, the target, again in parallel, acknowledges the write request back to the iSCSI initiator, which notifies the operating system. In other words, one cycle after sending the IO write request, the acknowledgement is received, and the OS and the associated application can continue along their merry way. This can be thought of as a fast IO acknowledgement release.

The process is multi-threaded at this point, or put another way, IO processing is parallelized and is using multi-processing. Because of that, the serialized bond described in IO processing earlier, where an application is put on hold waiting for the latency of an IO subsystem, with all of the performance issues that creates, is now unchained.

As described in the section on file fragmentation (page 23), also at play are the benefits of significantly reducing the probability of actually having to push an IO to the storage array because of deduplication. But even in the case where a write IO does have to de-stage, with fragmented write optimization and compression, the total number of IOs could be reduced from some 49 IOs to 1 or 2.

Just a reminder, the high hit rate read IO will also already be in deduplicated SSD. That also significantly reduces the number of IOs traversing the distance from the server to the storage array.

With that, we now have the answer to the IO gap problem. The amount of IO is reduced to pre-virtualization levels on the available IO paths.

As a result, applications like VDI, databases, and stream computing are able to rapidly continue without unnecessary process delays or latency.

Performance without tuning.

Storage Efficiency

The new IO architecture inline deduplication does not hold up performance like a solid state or rotational disk alone does, it accelerates it. Deduplication runs in parallel, as does destaging changed compressed and optimized blocks of data that must be written out to any tier of storage.

Because data is deduplicated, the total amount of data that must actually be moved to a storage subsystem is also significantly reduced. This has two benefits, the necessary storage capacity may be reduced by as much as 98%, and so are the amounts of IOPs actually hitting the array. Again when the IO does have to happen, it is fragmentation optimized and compressed further reducing IOPs.

All of this transforms an inefficient stack into an IO accelerated stack, with a huge reduction in necessary storage and all associated costs.

With this simple to understand game changing technology, the converged infrastructure performance requirements for the huge growth in virtualized IO demand is now possible, and the huge growth caused by big data scales, yet is contained, optimized and cost affordable.

A New IO Architecture Assisting BIG DATA and Database

The new IO architecture must include another technology that is unique and powerful to assist databases and Big Data. Deduplicated Snapshot Replication.

Snapshotting technology is not new and is widely used today. It has become an indispensible technology. It is used in almost every primary storage system available today.

But, deduplicated snapshot replication is something completely new altogether. Here is an example to understand it.

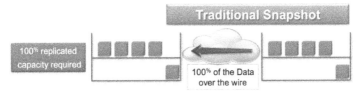

Consider a storage system that contains a copy of a virtual desktop, represented by a red block. As data often does and for this example using Virtual Desktops, we could make clones of that data, which are represented by the multiple data blocks above the original image.

In an ordinary storage system and in order to replicate the red blocks to a secondary storage system, a storage admin would create a snapshot, in order to freeze the contents of that data.

Then using a network, the data is transmitted to the replica system, which creates an identical copy on the other side and within the replica storage system.

As time passes and new blocks are added to the storage system, in a traditional storage system, all of these new blocks would appear as unique and duplicated-blocks. In order to replicate those blocks, we have to take another snapshot, and once again transmit all of them across the wire.

The problem with all of this is that is extremely inefficient. It consumes lots of storage, and it was necessary to send all of those replicas across a network when actually the original was already on the destination storage system.

The new IO architecture proposes to take deduplicated snapshots with a more intelligent and sophisticated approach than traditional snapshots. The new IO architecture would take a baseline snapshot, which is the original red block, later a secondary snapshot would be taken to capture new blocks that may have been cloned, then the new IO architecture performs a very fast comparison between the baseline snapshot, which has already been transmitted, and the secondary snapshot.

The new IO architecture doesn't just compare these blocks to see if they are new, they compare the blocks to see if they are unique.

As a result, only the unique blocks would be sent. In this case, the new IO architecture deduplicated snapshot replication would send what the new IO architecture might call a hollow block.

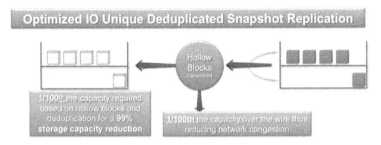

The hollow blocks are received on the other side and the data structure in what the new IO architecture would see as "rehydrated" to represent what a full snapshot replication would look like.

The big difference, however, is that the new IO architecture hollow blocks occupy only one one-hundredth of the size of the original blocks in the storage system. That translates into a 99% reduction in required replica storage. By using one one-hundredth of the network bandwidth to perform routine replications, The new IO architecture can save a great deal of the expense associated with data protection in both storage capacity and required bandwidth to transmit it.

This enhances, accelerates, and enables the idea of off-site data transmission, which would otherwise be both time and cost prohibitive.

The Bottom Line

All in all, the proposed new IO architecture could be a remarkable yet evolutionary technology - solving difficult problems with previously proven technology that together has the appearance and net effect of simplicity in its true form.

With this approach, the timeless IO performance gap issue has an answer. The over purchase of capacity to address both storage growth, and parallelizing paths to meet performance objectives also has an answer. Built in management technology must also be added in the stack such as thin provisioning enhanced and efficient snapshots, as well as VAAI.

The new IO architecture as an enhancement in the converged infrastructure stack at the IO layer could be a powerful game changing technology.

Recommended Actions

It's difficult to not think, there is good news and there is bad news.

On the negative side of things, there is no single company that has adequately addressed the issues of the IO performance gap issue. The industry at large, seems to be charging down a path that leads to the brick wall. There are people that most certainly understand that the brick wall is out there. But the hype and circumstances pressing the evolution of convergence seem to outweigh the need to solve this problem.

On the positive side of things, there are a variety of companies that have pieces of the solution today. Terrific zero delay deduplication, hollow-block snapshots, RAM cached IO, and defragmented efficient writing to external storage as examples.

The problem is that much like the whole Open System era, the end-user is left to cobble together a specific solution that may or may not replicate on another system.

The concept of convergence is to ultimately solve all of that. Users need to be asking their vendors to explain how they intend to avoid the IO performance brick wall.

To be the master of your own fate when architecting solutions today, IT professionals should consider:

1. The real capacity and performance needs of the data infrastructure and the impact of implementing that in a virtual environment

    a. Implementation decisions should balance performance and cost

2. Assess technology choices that provide modularity and price/performance leadership

3. Assess DeDupe, compression, and defragmentation alternatives

4. Assess storage technologies that can provide cached IO with effective use of DRAM and FLASH storage components in hierarchical real-time without overwhelming storage arrays with backend IO

To stave off the implications of the IO Performance Gap, ask vendors if they have:

1. Acceleration up the stack to applications and operating systems from the IO layer

    a. IO fast release, 1 cycle acknowledgment - providing DDR3 IO performance from SSD

    b. Hot data caching - automatically creating auto tiering benefits without migrating volumes around

   c. No need to vMotion storage for better performance, which only causes more storage related processing latency because of congestion in storage backend IO that is already swamped with other VM initiated traffic

2. Zero Latency in-line deduplication

   a. This could be a BIG benefit and it scales to match the needs of the converged data center (zetabytes) with no incremental processing penalties

3. IO reducing defragmented and compressed efficient writes.

4. Deduplicated snapshot replication

   a. reduces storage by 99% and it reduces what is transmitted across a wire (local or remote) by 99%

5. Thin provisioning

6. VAAI compliance

Summary

The next big swing of the IT evolutionary bat, is really a refinement to the strategy, objectives and path we have been on[12].

At the highest level, the convergence strategy strives to bridge the gap between business leaders, their objectives, and how IT goes about meeting those objectives to grow the business topline securely, while maintaining cost efficiencies for bottom line management.

The implementation of convergence is about deeper and better methodologies and technologies for consolidation[13], virtualization of everything, and most importantly centralized management across hybrid clouds to meet not only the remaining issues from the past, but also the emerging trends of the future that are driving the need for new tools and solutions designed to meet new IT demands like enterprise class support of mobile devices wherever they happen to be.

[12] Converged/integrated systems showed growth and density-optimized machines also grew – IDC thinks these machines had 26.6 per cent revenue growth to $735m in the Q1 2013 against just under 200,000 unit shipments

[13] "Mainstream SMB and enterprise server customers around the world continue to focus on consolidation, virtualization, and migration initiatives aimed at increasing efficiency and lowering datacenter infrastructure costs," said Matt Eastwood, general manager of enterprise platforms at IDC in a statement accompanying the statistics.

Emerging objectives and technologies strives to create a foundation that delivers cloud-era participation and multi-way collaboration from the myriad mobile devices IT is now tasked to support and manage with enterprise class application.

The emerging IT infrastructure will embrace mobility, social media, all of the legacy business applications modern businesses are built on, but also add analytics for real time processing or stream computing matching the velocity of data with analytically derived insights that will yield business growth, optimization and advantage. Complementing existing data warehouses, it will create a structure and query capability for unstructured and semi-structured data known as Big Data.

In the end, the next phase of IT infrastructure is not a small evolutionary step, it is one giant leap, with an impact so large that it is difficult to accurately quantify.

One thing is certain, it will be the platform for the near future, and it will be the basis from which new technologies will be integrated into, because there will be no major changes in strategic direction for the foreseeable future, only refinements.

Until now, there has been no cost efficient way to scale performance and storage capacity to even meet current demands, with the increased demands of converged infrastructures being beyond reasonable if not imagination.

Development of a new IO architecture could be a solution that augments the converged infrastructure architecture with an IO layer solution that is elegantly simply, and targets the performance choke point between servers and storage in the IO path, while significantly reducing all storage needs.

The new IO architecture could deliver transformational economics. Business leaders would enjoy increased investment capital, allowing for performance and efficiency in developing new offerings rapidly, while users would be satisfied with performance, wherever they may be.

The new IO architecture would be uniquely reliable, fast and cost effective. Enough to satisfy any enterprise - a combination that stands alone in value and would surely accelerate the growth and use of Big Data, and Data Mobility through hybrid cloud services everywhere.

About the Author

Randall Chalfant is a Fellow of IABPro, which provides world-class consulting for professionally managed industry advisory boards. Chalfant's domain expertise includes: storage, mainframes, open system servers, operating systems, applications and networking solutions, and business development.

Recently, he was the VP of Strategy at Nexsan, where he formed key strategic storage alliances that lead to significant market share and company growth. He is an industry speaker, and has authored a multitude of technical whitepapers and financial calculators.

Prior to Nexsan, he was the CTO at Sun Microsystems and StorageTek, and held various marketing, engineering development and executive management positions at Network Systems, Data Switch, Amdahl, and Trilogy Systems. Chalfant is a visionary and lecturer, and resides in the suburbs of Denver with his wife of 39 years.